Never Mind the Pain

Michelle Williamson

Presentation by *BookLeaf Publishing*

Web: www.bookleafpub.com

E-mail: info@bookleafpub.com

ISBN: 9789358737363

First edition 2023

I'd like to dedicate this book to several people. One being my daughter, Chyenne Marie. When you were born was one of the greatest days of my life, and the day I began to breathe again. You gave me the will to live again. I love you my dear girl.

William, I know I say a lot that I would have fallen apart without you these last few years, but I know you know different. I know, you just needed to be by my side as I pulled myself together. And for that I will be forever grateful. Thank you, my love.

Lastly, but not at all least; my son Dakota Scott. May your soul rest easy in the afterlife my sweet Bear. Mama Loves you.

ACKNOWLEDGEMENT

Without certain people in my life, I would not have pushed myself to finally pursue my dream. To Ms. D. Brasfield, Mrs.P. Doty, Mrs.C. English, and Mr. D. Schanou; all former teachers of mine that saw something in me when at times I did see them in myself. From the bottom of my heart, thank you for believing in me.

To Sarah McIntosh, thank you for always being one of my greatest friends growing up and in the becoming family. I love you, Sis.

Battle scarred and broken

Battle scarred and broken.
A wounded soul.
Do not trust what you cannot control.
A soul that is broken is scarred to the core,
healing is a long time coming for a battered soul.
Heed what you do not know,
The rest is in tow.
Be careful of the hardened heart that leads to the
soul.
You may not like what you find behind closed
doors.
The heart has secrets in store,
that will shock and surprise to the core.
Beware of the wall around the heart,
it will not easily fall.
Only another battle scarred, and broken soul can
heal the scars and wounds within.
Hail to the kindred spirit within,
that's makes you strong enough to survive the
trials of a murderous life.
Continue battling your demons,
The worst has passed.
You will conquer all,
the spirit and Goddess within you deems it so.
Wounded, Battle Scarred and Broken no more.

As You Look into My Eyes

As you look into my eyes, I wonder what it is that you see.

Do you see the real me or me at all?

I have always wondered what it is that you see.

When I look into the mirror, I see me but not the real me.

I still see the fear, anger, and frustration of living with the person who hurt me

But I also see the love I have for everyone else.

I look into your eyes as you look into mine

I do not see or hear anything in the way you look at me or the way you speak to me.

There is nothing, but yet something, you just will not let me reach you.

Are you scared of telling or showing me how
you feel about what you see.

By doing this you don't let me know if you care,
love, fear or if you are frustrated by me.

How am I supposed to know?

When you look into my eyes are you seeing
what is killing me inside?

Do you even care?

Do you see all the things I don't want you to
see?

Or the things I do?

Tell me!!!

I also wonder if you realize I'm here.

Alive?

Do you realize the suffering I am going through?

As you look into my eyes do you see anything at all?

I have tried so many times and so hard to have you see what it is that I see, on the other side of the mirror.

And it bothers me that cannot or will not see the things that make me,

But if you happen to just once, only once and that is it. That would mean so much.

So, do you see anything?

Anything at all?

If so and you do not want to see me, just simply walk away.

Because I really do not want you to see what you do not want to see.

See the fear, anger, love, frustration, or most of all the pain that I go through each day.

So do not look or speak to me if you do not want
to see all these things that make me.

That makes me who I am

But if you genuinely care and love me, you look
into these pain filled eyes.

Anger and Rage

All my anger and all my pain turn to rage, God forbid it come out on you.

Please forgive me. I never meant to hurt anyone.

I cannot seem to find myself anymore; I have been lost among the wreckage of the past.

I have no idea where to go from here.

So, lost.

So, much pain.

So much anger.

So much rage that I just break.

How do I let go?

Let go of what has kept me going all these years.

What is my life without it?

Help me find my way.

Someone catch me as I fall.

Hate You

You, you sorry son of a bitch!

You single handily destroyed my life to where I could not regain control.

How could you be so cruel?

I HATE YOU!

You are a bastard, a hateful cruel bastard.

You took my sanity, my control, my life.

I HATE YOU!

I hate everything you stand for.

I hate everything you do.

I hate how you are mean, even more when you're nice.

You think you can be nice to me and all that you did will go away.

It won't!

I HATE YOU!

I trusted you, and you betrayed me.

How dare you?

I Hate you!

You molested me, you beat me, you raped me.

I HATE YOU!

I hope you die a slow painful death, and my face
is the last thing you see when you are sent to
hell.

You are a selfish condescending bastard.

I HATE YOU!

You will destroy my life no more!!!!

Have fun in hell you fucking bastard!

I still feel you

Though you are gone.

I still feel you

in certain places of the house, in the ways that people look at me, and when I hear a song that reminds me of you.

Though you're gone, I can still feel you.

I feel you around me when I'm happy, sad, or extremely mad.

I still feel you.

I miss you!

I have always wondered why, why you left?

Why did you decide to take your life?

You left us, left us all alone, in this cruel hateful world that just doesn't understand us.

Why?

I still feel you,

while looking at pictures I see what all of us
used to be,

and I think of what could have been.

I still feel you, so do a lot of people.

Sometimes I cry myself to sleep, but I know that
you are watching over me making sure that I am
all right.

Four years later,

I still feel your presence around me,

and that makes me feel safe when no one else
does.

Just Breathe

Just Breathe

I'm beaten down and cold

just breathe

I'm out of the loop, trying to piece everything
back together

just breathe

I've been kicked and thrown around

just breathe

I am no longer laying down to be trampled on

just breathe

here and now,

I stand and fight and I say to myself to start over
and to....

JUST BREATHE

Without You

Eighteen years ago, you left.

Left before I was born, not knowing who I was,
or what I wanted out of life.

For so many years I did not know I had a father,
didn't know that I could ask about you.

I didn't even know my own father's name; I
knew nothing of a father.

Thirteen years old I finally got the courage to
ask about you.

I had a name and that was about it.

Months later I am handed a letter.

Addressed to a Miss Michelle Williamson

It was from my daddy, you, you finally wrote to
me.

I almost fell to the floor.

My heart was racing, and my head was spinning.

Before I even opened the letter, I had tears in my
eyes.

I opened it, a three-to-four-page letter with two
pictures.

I had a face to go with a name.

I also had a sister.

A sister that I never knew I had.

I was part of a family and didn't know it.

I'm seventeen now, I have done ok without you.

But I did need you, but you weren't around to
help.

Help with the emotional, mental, and physical scars that I have had to endure.

Days gone by, I still wish to know my father, the man who gave me life.

The father I never knew I had.

But I want to know everything there is to know about you.

Especially why you left.

That hurt most of all.

Although I have learned to control the hurt to where it doesn't hurt as much, it still hurts.

But you see our story doesn't quiet end yet.

May 14th, 2000, I will meet my father, the man who gave me life, but then somehow destroyed it.

It'll get better, someday.

17 ½ years later I'll meet my father for the first time.

I cannot wait, 'till then my heart will sit and wonder what it would have been like to be a part of your life, and you a part of mine.

Give Me A Voice

Childlike, quiet, scared, and small turned inward
without a voice because no one would listen

Why won't you listen

Oh, goddess give me a voice

Holding everything inside because right now
that is stifled, it's broken

Insecurities and memories of our monster

Oh, goddess give me a voice

As a teenager the written word catches your eye
and peaks a desire

It blossoms and sets a foundation inside of your
soul

Words have now become so much more

Before they were just sentences to explain the
unknown.

Now, oh now.

Now it is to set you in a place and make you feel
what is around you. What has become of your
heart. Because your written word is your heart.
It has been since it left its mark on your soul.

Oh, dear goddess give me a voice

As you have grown older you know that the
Goddess has granted your wish long ago.
Because look dear girl, look how you write...you
have your voice

Unlearn

How do I unlearn what put me in survival mode?

Unlearn what it means to be abused

Unlearn what it means to be molested

Unlearn what it means to be raped

Unlearn not to flinch when someone walks into a room

Unlearn how not to freak out when someone raises their voice

How do I unlearn having a panic attack from having a C-PTSD trigger

How do I unlearn the fear of a generation of men that has absolutely nothing to do with my torment except for the one man who decided to take something I was unwilling to give?

How do I unlearn all that bullshit that is shoved
down a survivor's throat of it all just takes time.
Blah blah blah.

How do I unlearn that my monster was supposed
to be a trusted person in my life

How do I unlearn all of the hurt that you put all
of our family through.

Years and years of torment.

Even if you aren't around

Your insidious voice is still in our heads makes
our lives miserable

It's hard to unlearn the monster when it's seared
into the corners of my mind and the depths of
my soul

How do I unlearn you

For sanities sake

I hope there is an answer

ERMS - Cancer The Silent Killer

ERMS

Embryonal Rhabdomyosarcoma

Cancer the Silent Killer

Four letters of a death sentence

Four years of treatment, recovery, illness, hospitals, health. Surgeries and hospital stays.

ERMS

Four letters of a death sentence

Chemo, Radiation, C-diff.

IV Poles, Medications, and isolation.

Cancer the Silent Killer

ERMS

Four letters of a death sentence

Scans, Scans, and more Scans

And finally...

REMISSION

But...Remember

Cancer is the Silent Killer

ERMS

Four letters to a death Sentence

Two years of remission...

Gone in a flash

Cancer the Silent Killer

ERMS

Four letters to a death sentence

A trip to the ER confirmed our worst fears

Surgeries, Hospitals, Chemo.

Pain.

All of it.

All over...

Again...

Cancer the Silent Killer

ERMS

Four letters to a death sentence

One Major Surgery

Three Hospitals

One Last Wish

One Loving Commitment Ceremony

One Last Birthday

One Last Conversation

One Last I love you

One Final Breath

ERMS

Four Letters to a Death Sentence

Cancer the Silent Killer

M.W.

Oct.

1st, 2023

I Washed My Hair

I washed my hair today

Such a small feat for most but such an enormous
one for me. Because you see it's been getting
bad again.

Not sleeping, not eating, not being present.

But

I washed my hair today

It had been a while, takin care of myself was
never priority

Life was a mess

I was a mess

But

I washed my hair today

Being under the water melted the past few days

The shot nerves from the hour and half
meltdown from the day before that just drained
absolutely everything out of me.

All that rage just unleashed over something that
could have been prevented and in the whole of
everything is so small.

But, at least

I washed my hair today

Getting rid of those raw emotions down the
drain feels like heaven and as I step out of the
shower, I start to feel somewhat normal

Getting dressed and feeling more human
Looking in the mirror

I smile and say

there you are

Welcome back Michelle

All because

I washed my hair today

Losing You

Losing You

I find I am at constant war with myself.

I never know when I'll have a good day or bad.
I'm either angry or sad.

I've tried to control the emotions, but I find
that's an ever-ending nightmare.

I wear your ashes in a necklace every day to
have that closeness that I miss so much.

I'd give anything for a "Bear" hug.

I never understood why a child of any age had to
fight against such a deadly Dease

Oh, Baby Bear losing you made me question so
many things in life.

Losing you has so many effects and also
knowing what you would never have me very
bitter.

No Prom

No Graduation

No College

No Wife

No Children

No life after Cancer

So, losing you was a new perspective

From raising you for 17 years to having you be
gone in a matter of days.

Walking into Hospice, knowing we weren't
walking out.

Was one of the absolute hardest things I've ever
done.

Losing you

Hearing you breathe was torture, especially as it
got worse throughout the night.

The death rattle is something you never forget.

Just imagine it coming from child.

Now you know part of my nightmare.

Part of the why, "Can't sleep"

I slept for maybe an hour and half,

Somehow you knew that was what I needed
before the fallout coming my way

Before I laid down, I spoke to you, I hadn't
heard your voice in a few days so I had hope you
would hear me

I told you that I loved you and that it was okay
to let go.

That somehow, someway that all of us would be
okay. We all loved and still love you so very
much.

But we didn't want you in pain in any longer. I
kissed your forehead and laid down.

Losing you

I felt defatted and so down

I held you as you took your last breaths, your
grandmother and Great-Aunt held me.

I helped with your last bath and got a final lock
of your hair.

Oh, Baby Bear

Losing Your

Broke Me

I gave you one final forehead kiss; said I love
you and goodbye

The next time I held you it felt surreal.

I mean, I was holding an urn.

How could this be my son?

Losing you

Moving forward has slow going and sometimes
not at all.

Good days and bad

Days to where I see a picture of you, and it will
bring me the greatest joy. Or the ones where it
will bring me to my knees and knock the wind
out of me.

Losing you Baby Bear

Has been the worst pain I've ever felt.

Karma

Ever mind the rule of three

Whatever you put forth comes back to thee

Times three...

I have always followed the rules and so it is with
Karma that I know that you will be taken care
of, and I hope I am around it comes for you

All the damage you've done

All the lives you've destroyed

And you don't ever know

Don't even care

Oh Karma

Ever mind the Rule of Three

It's going to bite you in the ass, and you have only yourself to blame. Yes, abuse does run down the family, but you could have ended it!

You could have chosen differently!

But NO! No, you chose to indulge in your sickness and come after me and others.

So.. Oh yes Karma will come for you and that will be my salvation.

When Love and Hate Collide

What happens when love and hate collide?

The pain you feel in both aspects is unbelievable, unbearable, inconceivable, and totally heart wrenching.

You have no idea which side to choose when you need it the most.

I lived my life in hate for so long I didn't notice it anymore.

Now, I know it for what it is and what it was... A mistake.

I should never have hated the man who made me miserable, but then again how and why could I love him?

The answer is unknown to me.

Life goes on its path to destiny, and we will see what the future brings to me.

Love, Hate, Happiness, Sorrow.

No one knows for sure, except the Gods and
goddesses.

As for now they hold my future in their hands,
but not my past.

That is now in my hands.

And I plan with all my might to throw my
deepest darkest demons away into oblivion,
where they may rest and find peace.

When they find peace, my heart, mind, and soul
won't hurt so much anymore.

I can forgive, but I will never forget.

That's what happens when love and hate collide.

Too Hard to Deal With

Your daughter, my best friend, said you had
cancer.

I thought you weren't going to die.

Not so soon anyway.

I mean that just could not happen.

Not to my father figure, not to you.

Renae just called.

I screamed!

Mom and dad took the phone and just held me
there for several minutes.

I kept crying and screaming I couldn't stop.

You were gone?!

You left Sarah and me behind.

Why?

It's about a year later and it still hurts so much.

To even think about you makes me cry.

As I sit here and write this, I am crying.

Not so long ago the family has started moving things out of the house for someone new to live there.

In the place where I basically grew up.

Paul, even though you're gone, I keep you, father, in my heart

Every day, Always!

GOODBYE DADDY

Scared

I had just woken up; it was Monday morning.

I was hoping, just hoping that what happened yesterday had just been a bad nightmare, but to my horror as I looked into the mirror, I realized that it wasn't or hadn't been the nightmare I was hoping for.

It was all real.

I wanted to die right then and there.

As I looked into the mirror, I saw someone different, someone who didn't or should not belong there, you see, I didn't see me well not the old me. I saw a different person, a person who had bruises all over her face, someone who was scared, hurt, and mortified. I was hurt physically, emotionally, and mentally.

As I was walking out of the front door to go to
the bus stop, my mother stopped me and said, "I
love you and I'm so very sorry." Walking to the
bus stop I was thinking to myself, why should
she be sorry, she didn't hurt me, beat me, or do
anything to me. Why should she be sorry?

At the bus stop some of the kids didn't know
how to act. Some made fun, and others stood
there too scared to say or do anything. A half
hour later the Sheriff and a lady from the Social
Services department came to see me. They
asked a lot of questions and then took me to the
police station. I was so scared; I didn't know
what to do. I was shaking and sweating, inside
and out. And crying. Crying because I no idea
what was going to happen to me.

When I was there, two class periods left in the
school day. They let me go back to class; but
everyone was at P.E., and they didn't make me
go. I was kind of glad. When everybody got to
class, they understood what I was going through
or they were just too scared to say anything.

With one class left, I was called back to the office. I was still scared but I walked to the office anyway. The Social Services lady said I would be going to a place called BoysTown it was in Grand Island, about 23 miles away from my home, my mother, and my little brother. I was really scared.

At this point I was very scared, because I was going to be in a strange place, with strange people and away from the security of my own room. My bed, by house, my family.

When I got there, everybody was really nice, and I didn't feel so bad anymore. The kids and the staff were really friendly, and they didn't ask or say anything about the bruises all over my face. I'm quite sure they understood. So, it helped, and I was happy because I wasn't scared. The people were cool and most all I wasn't going to get hurt by anyone anymore.

A Cry For Momma

Yesterday you said you loved me; I said the same.

You had an appointment in G.I. the next day.

One that would change our lives forever.

I went to school before you got home from work, so I didn't get to say anything,

anything at all.

Katherine brought me home; I was ready to walk into the house; but I stopped dead in my tracks.

I almost dropped my things, there was a note on the door:

Michelle don't forget to feed and water the cats, dog, and fish. Do you own laundry. Let Willy out before school, after school and at ten pm.

Dad (Victor) will call you later.

I love you!

MOM.

That note changed me, made me see, made me
feel pain.

I hate that damned note.

I called him, he said he had something to tell
me, something he could not and would not tell
me over the phone.

I called Sara, I wasn't myself, I was gone.

But that damn door wouldn't close, it wasn't
going to let me shut out the world anymore.

She came over to be with me.

Half hour later I heard the truck doors slam shut.

I opened the door, there stood Dad and Vicki.

He looked me straight in the eyes.

I knew, I knew you weren't coming home.

I somehow found the way to the chair and fell
into it,

then it struck like a knife in my heart.

The pain and tears,

my mom was gone.

Days later you called to say you were all right
and to check up on me.

I knew you weren't coming home for awhile,

you were getting help, getting better so we could
be a family again, as messed up as that family
was.

When The Nightmares Come Alive

I woke up screaming in a cold sweat, sitting
straight up looking around the room wide eyed
in a state of panic.

The nightmare was alive, so real, so undeniably
vivid.

I take a deep breath and let it out slowly as I sink
back against the pillows, closing my eyes to the
pain, trying so desperately not to let the tears
fall.

Tears that I vowed would never be shed.

But why when the nightmare came alive?

I remember every sight, every sound,
every...bruise.

Every nightmare I ever had has come alive.

Just put me out of my misery.

But no. Life isn't that easy.

I would rather watch the nightmares come alive night after night than give up the fight for my life.

Nightmares that come alive or not, you realize that every life isn't always a nightmare.

The Rain

The rain keeps falling like tears from my soul,

Down the stream of heartache.

Remembering what happened to me and how it
all destroyed me.

It only makes me weep in pain.

The rain will never stop.

What happened is now in the past but will
forever be imbedded in my mind.

In the future I will let it out.

Even though the rain, full of my tears still falls,
it doesn't hurt quiet as much anymore.

But the hurt is still there.

While I cry myself to sleep, everything goes through my mind, and I realize that the rain will never stop.

How can the rain stop if the tears don't stop?

They won't, they will fall forever and ever.

The drops as well as the rain are still falling to this day.

Never Mind The Pain

Never mind the pain

Never mind the part of me that is broken

Never mind the seething rage buried deep inside
of me

Never mind all the times I've screamed bloody
murder for the torment to stop

Never mind the endless nights of sleep that seem
to come

and are always so often

Never mind how many times I've cried myself
to sleep wanting it all,

the nightmare itself to end

Never mind how it all replays itself in my mind
time after time on an endless loop

Never mind that my mind is fragmented

Never mind how I will never be the same

Just…. Never mind me.

3-17-09

www.ingramcontent.com/pod-product-compliance
Lightning Source LLC
LaVergne TN
LVHW050938200726
843508LV00011B/2371